Good
Manners
in Minutes

Emilie Barnes

HARVEST HOUSE PUBLISHERS
EUGENE, OREGON

Cover photos © iStockphoto / senkonate; Danny Smythe / Big Stock Photo

Cover by Dugan Design Group, Bloomington, Minnesota

GOOD MANNERS IN MINUTES
Copyright © 2010 by Emilie Barnes
Published by Harvest House Publishers
Eugene, Oregon 97402
www.harvesthousepublishers.com

ISBN 978-0-7369-2992-9

16 17 / BP-SK / 10 9 8 7 6

Contents

The Heart of Manners

Creating a Welcoming Home

*A*re you surprised that a book on manners begins with your home? Good manners are all about making people feel comfortable and cared for. And the first thing visitors see when they come to visit is your house and property. What first impression are you making? Will your guests feel relaxed? Are you setting the foundation so they'll know your home is one of peace and harmony, where good manners are a priority? When you take care of your home, those who live there and those who visit know they too will be cared for.

A pleasing home is not measured by perfection. Instead, it's measured by the gracious style you've established. Make your home neat, with a swept sidewalk leading to the front door. A potted flowering plant is always a welcoming sign for your guests and your family.

The personality of a welcoming home makes guests want to linger, regardless of whether the home is a hut or a palace. And please don't feel stressed if your home isn't decorated exactly like you want it to be right now. Remember, a home is always in process. If you wait to invite guests until everything is perfect or close to it, you will never have company.

Two Important Ingredients

*I*f you want to discover how to create a welcoming home, there is no better classroom about the joining of hospitality and social graces than a visit to the southern United States. This culture has earned its "Southern hospitality" reputation. I've had the good fortune to visit Charleston, South Carolina, and Savannah, Georgia, and in both cities I experienced the great feeling of "Welcome to our lifestyle." The South shines as a model when it comes to grace, charm, and guest care. It's a place where people even slow down a bit from their hectic pace of life to enjoy the ritual of afternoon tea—one of my favorite things! This section of the United States still honors social poise and presentation. Grandmother's china cups and silver elements are reverenced. The table is covered with a crisp tablecloth instead of plastic and the good china is used instead of paper plates. Table manners are alive and well, even among the young.

The ingredients of hospitality and social graces go naturally together. You might use different elements and different languages, but wherever you are, those two ingredients make a winning recipe.

5 Great Traits to Nurture

A person who exhibits kindness and warmth and good manners reflects his or her commitment to the "Golden Rule," to treating others as he or she would like to be treated. People who care about manners usually exhibit and nurture these characteristics and values: tact, respect, self-confidence, flexibility, and common sense. These traits are important in everyday relationships and within families, where respectful and considerate behavior cements the bonds of love and affection. What do these traits indicate?

> *Tactful:* Mannerly people who value honesty and realize they needn't be brutally frank when talking with others. Thoughtless words can hurt, so people with tact guard their tongues.
>
> *Respectful:* When there are different opinions about issues, people with respect listen to the opinions of others and don't get into

arguments. If there is a strong, critical disagreement, respectful people schedule a time when they can speak with the people they disagree with to discuss the issues in private. Respecting differing points of view creates stronger relationships and broadens horizons.

Self-confident: Well-mannered people are self-assured and clearly communicate with others, even during demanding and difficult circumstances. Confidence enables grace to exist under pressure.

Flexible: People who value manners understand that etiquette is an expression of cultural and social values and respect is important. This means they willingly modify their manners and behavior (within reason) to accommodate the traditions and beliefs of others.

Commonsense: People who believe in good manners know how to facilitate good relations with others by adapting to the needs of others without sacrificing their own values. They know how to make proper etiquette a natural part of daily living.

If your beliefs, actions, and behaviors reflect these traits, you will be able to function very well in all kinds of social situations and settings.

A Fun "True or False" Quiz

*B*efore getting into the nitty-gritty on manners, why not take a few minutes and assess how well you know the basics? If you're like me, you might be surprised how casual you've become about good manners. Circle your answer to each question.

1. If you aren't sure which utensil to use at a social gathering, watch the host or hostess, essentially "following the leader."

    True   False

2. It's okay to talk on your cell phone when in a restaurant.

    True   False

3. You should check with the host before you bring your children to a social event.

    True   False

4. When dining out, it's okay to blow your nose or lightly touch up makeup at the table.

    True   False

5. When setting the table, the salad fork is placed
   to the left of the dinner fork.

   True   False

6. At dinner, if the person next to you is busy,
   you can reach around his or her plate to get
   the basket of bread if you can do so without
   knocking anything over and say, "Excuse me."

   True   False

7. If you need to use a toothpick to dislodge food
   between your teeth, you should excuse yourself and go to someplace private.

   True   False

8. In today's busy world, you don't have to send a
   thank-you card when you receive a gift.

   True   False

9. At dinner you should butter your entire piece
   of bread at one time. It saves energy and is
   more convenient.

   True   False

10. When setting the table, the dinner knife goes
    to the right of the plate, sharp edge facing out.

    True   False

11. When at the table, food is always passed to the left (clockwise).

    True   False

12. It's acceptable to send a thank-you note via e-mail or text message.

    True   False

13. When planning a social event, send out the invitations one week before the date so people won't have time to forget.

    True   False

14. When leaving the table during the meal, place your napkin on your chair.

    True   False

15. Your cell phone should be set on vibrate when you're at church or a social function so you don't disturb the speakers or the people around you.

    True   False

16. Casual (but not sloppy) attire is acceptable for funerals, Sunday church, and weddings.

    True   False

17. If you can't find a babysitter for your young
    children, you can still go to a social event, but
    make sure you sit in the back so you can leave
    if your kids get unruly.

    True   False

18. It's no longer necessary for a man to hold
    the door, pull out a chair at dinner, or offer a
    woman other similar courtesies. The basic con-
    cept and accompanying actions are obsolete.

    True   False

19. A gentleman should not offer to shake hands
    with a lady unless she extends her hand first.

    True   False

20. To signal the waiter that you're finished with
    your meal, place your knife and fork across
    your plate, going from the nine o'clock to the
    three o'clock position.

    True   False

Answers

1. True	11. False
2. False	12. False
3. True	13. True
4. False	14. False
5. True	15. True
6. False	16. False
7. True	17. True
8. False	18. False
9. False	19. True
10. False	20. False

Scoring

Count the number of correct answers and refer to the scores below.

0-5: You really need this book. *Help!*

6-10: You missed out on some essential manner lessons so this refresher course is perfect for you.

11-15: You're on the right track, but more is to be learned.

16-18: You're doing a good job overall so now you get to do some fine-tuning.

19-20: Go to the head of the class! You'll still enjoy this book. Reviewing good manners is always good.

Good manners sometimes means simply putting up with other people's bad manners.

H. JACKSON BROWN, JR.

Gracious Entertaining

Me Entertain? No Way!

Many people go to restaurants or other public venues to meet others. They don't entertain at home because, well, there are many excuses:

- → I'm too busy to entertain.

- → My young children prevent me from having guests at home.

- → My home is too small.

- → I don't have the proper serving dishes.

- → I can't find good help to assist me.

- → I'm not very good in the kitchen.

- → I can't seem to coordinate all the elements so that everything comes together at the same time.

At one time or another we've all uttered one of these excuses. If you need a great excuse *to* entertain, here's a good one: We need to be around other people. God built into us a need for fellowship.

Entertaining helps us get out of our ruts so we can experience doing something different for a change.

Entertaining 101

Although we don't want to get caught up in all the subtle nuances of high-society rules and regulations, there are some tried-and-true ways of doing things—including how to invite people, how to set the table, and how to serve the food. If you didn't grow up around social gatherings or haven't had many opportunities to extend social graces to guests, you might be intimidated about entertaining.

When you think "entertain," what comes to mind? Do you envision a huge gala or a very elegant evening with gourmet food, fancy decorations, and a hired wait staff? That would be delightful, yes, but how often does this occur in your life? Probably not often. And there are many, many versions and options when it comes to hosting a gathering at your home.

My motto is "Don't say I can't do that." I encourage you to make it yours too. When contemplating entertaining, start simple. Begin small. Have one or two people over for a meal or a movie. It's that simple. In fact, you're probably already realizing this great secret: You may already be entertaining without realizing it. Have you invited a small group to your home for a book club and conversation? That's entertaining. Have you had a neighbor or friend over for a cup of tea and a scone? That's entertaining. Have you hosted a barbecue for some neighbors in your backyard? That's entertaining. Have you put on a birthday party for one of your children? That's entertaining too.

Inviting People Over

$\mathcal{D}$ecide on a day to do something with someone and then set it up. Invitations can range from formal printed cards to casual invites at church or in the park. Starting small, you can gather people together by saying:

→ "Come on over after church on Sunday for brunch."

→ "Would you like to come over Friday afternoon at four for a cup of coffee or tea?"

→ "Our daughter is having her tenth birthday

party Tuesday after school, starting around four. She'd be delighted to have your daughter, Mary, attend. We hope she can come."

→ "Our big Fourth of July swim party is just around the corner. Your whole family is invited to join us for fun, food, and games."

The best guest list includes people with diversified backgrounds and interests. This helps create interesting conversations on a wide range of topics. And don't worry if everything isn't perfect or you feel you lack materially. It's not what you don't have that makes entertaining special. What's fascinating and worthwhile is what you do with what you have.

Special Invitations

Most people have become very casual in their approach to inviting someone to a dinner party. Casual seems to be a fashion statement! However, there will be certain occasions that call for a slightly more formal approach when inviting guests. Such an invitation might look like this:

Dear Jennifer,

Bob and I would love to have you and Bill as our guests for dinner at our home. We're

hoping you can come Friday evening,
November 3, at 6:30.

We look forward to seeing you if you can
come. Please let me know if that day and
time will work for you.

With love,
Emilie

Did you notice this invitation includes the place,
the date, and the time? It also asks for a confirmation.
The invitation does not include the day you wrote it or
planned to send it.

A semi-informal note of invitation is usually sent
out a week to ten days before the set date. Invitations to
very close friends may be sent five or so days in advance.
Formal invitations are usually sent ten days to three
weeks in advance. Everyone has busy calendars, so "the
sooner the better" is a good rule of thumb if you want
them to come.

An Informal Note of Acceptance or Regret

When you've been invited to a gathering, send your
acceptance or regrets as soon as possible so the host
will know how many people are coming. Responding
quickly to regrets is especially important because the
host may need to change the date or find other people

to fill out the party. Your response can be simple and straightforward:

> Dear Emilie,
>
> Thank you for your invitation for dinner. Unfortunately Bill and I have a previous engagement. We're so sorry, but we're glad you thought of us. Let's try again soon.
>
> Sincerely,
> Jennifer

When you're invited to an event, always RSVP within a week or by the timeline given. And never be a no-show if you've said you will attend.

Planning for Spontaneity?

*C*an you plan a party and still allow for spontaneity? Absolutely. It takes a certain amount of thinking ahead to make spontaneity in a group of people possible. If you're out somewhere or someone calls, don't hesitate to "spontaneously" invite them over. Why can you be so confident? Because you've done some general planning ahead of time.

One good preparation detail is to have flowers (silk

or real) and a pretty vase on hand. You can put together a quick and delightful bouquet for a cheery center-piece. If you have a freezer, you can make casseroles and appetizers in advance, freeze them, and then you'll always have something ready to serve in a pinch. Keep up with general housework by doing short, daily stints of tidying that will keep your house clean enough for an impromptu celebration.

What you keep on hand will truly save the day and open up your life to more celebrations and times of fellowship. Here are basic items to have on hand. By using these and combining them, you can make a walk-in visitor feel like a king or queen.

- ❖ berries, frozen
- ❖ biscuits (refrigerated)
- ❖ Bisquick
- ❖ bread dough, frozen
- ❖ brown sugar
- ❖ brownie mix
- ❖ butter
- ❖ cake mix, yellow
- ❖ chocolate chips
- ❖ cinnamon

- coconut, shredded
- coffee, regular and decaffeinated
- eggs
- flour
- fruit cocktail
- graham cracker crumbs
- instant pudding, vanilla
- juice, frozen
- marshmallows
- milk, sweetened condensed
- muffins
- nutmeg
- nuts
- pie crusts, ready-made
- pound cake, frozen
- raisins
- sour cream
- sugar
- tea, regular and herbal

You'll be surprised at how many wonderful opportunities to entertain will present themselves when you're prepared.

What's in a Name?

$\int$ ome people have the ability to retain and recall a person's name for years after their initial meeting. Others forget a person's name shortly after the first handshake. To be good with names has a lot of advantages. People are always impressed when you call them by name after not seeing them for a period of time. What will help you remember people?

While being introduced to someone, focus on his or her name. If a name is unusual, I often ask the person to spell it for me, which helps etch it into my memory. Another good technique for remembering is to write it down on a piece of paper and review it later or file it so you can go over a list of people that might be at the next similar event.

Name tags might seem silly initially, but they are very helpful for most people. Providing a visual representation of a person's name helps the name sink in. I find them very helpful when there is a large gathering with a mix of people from various groups and associations. If you have a holiday gathering and invite friends, coworkers, and neighbors, it is very helpful to provide the tags. They make it much easier to blend a large group and encourage conversation. You're helping to create an environment where your guests can relax and enjoy one another's company.

Setting place cards by each plate on the table is also helpful. Set them above the dinner plate at each person's place or on top of the napkin on the dinner plate. The cards are often plain white or ivory, but you can get creative and work the look into your dinner's theme (if there is one). Use your best penmanship to print your guest's name on the card or print them using decorative type.

Preparing for Guests

What you do in advance of greeting your guests will set the tone for their experience in your home. When the rooms are tidy and arranged for the comfort of your friends and family members, they will be able to relax and focus on conversation and community. Here are some great tips:

→ Be ready at least 30 minutes before your guests are expected to arrive. Nothing is more awkward for the guests than watching the host run around and tidy up.

→ If you have children, make sure their toys are picked up from the rooms you and your company will be using.

→ Fluff the sofa pillows, but don't place them
where your guests will worry about messing
them up.

→ The evening will go a lot smoother if you've
planned ahead of time for special touches. For
example, if it's wintertime, have logs in place
for a fire.

→ Be sure to put out a fresh bar of soap, guest
towels, and a scented candle in the bathroom
visitors will use.

→ Have umbrellas handy in case it rains so
departing guests can get to their cars without
getting wet.

A Welcoming Welcome

How you welcome your guests sets the tone for the
visit and also makes a lasting impression. So give
them your undivided attention in those first moments
at the door. That positive connection will last throughout your time together.

→ Greet guests at the door. Never holler,
"Come in!"

→ Ask to take coats and purses and put them in an easily accessible yet secure location.

→ Arrange beforehand what part your children will play in the evening. Children can help by greeting guests and taking their hats, purses, and coats. They can assist in serving the food and clearing the table. If it's an adults only event, have a plan in place for their evening too.

→ Introduce guests to the rest of the group. Make sure everyone knows each other. Don't forget to introduce any visiting children to adults and the other children. If it's a large gathering, provide name tags.

→ Escort your guests to the gathering place (living room, backyard, sunroom) and help them find a place to sit.

→ Offer them something to drink soon after their arrival.

→ If you have a special area for children, be sure to have someone show them the way and invite them to enjoy the playroom or area set up for them. A table in the corner set up with a craft or activity is a simple way to corral loud and rambunctious kids.

- ⤳ Prearrange the placement of your guests so strangers will get to know each other.

- ⤳ Have place cards on the table so your company will know where to sit.

- ⤳ If you're serving the food, remember to approach from the left.

- ⤳ When removing plates, approach from the right.

These basic guidelines will provide structure for your event and help make your company feel welcome.

I seek constantly to improve my manners and graces, for they are the sugar to which all are attracted.

OG MANDINO

Conversation Courtesies

Your Words Are Powerful

Words are powerful. They impact your spouse, kids, extended family members, coworkers, friends, and strangers who interact with you or are near you. How you communicate also influences how you feel and act. Positive words build up; negative words tear down. That may seem obvious, but sometimes we lose sight of how our words can be viewed.

Have you analyzed your word choices lately? Does your communication tend to be positive or negative? Let's take a quick self-evaluation. In each of the following pairs, circle the one you tend to use.

Positive Words	Negative Words
✦ I can	I can't
✦ I will	I'll try
✦ I want to	I have to

Positive Words	**Negative Words**
→ I will do	I should have
→ my goal	I could have
→ today	someday
→ next time	if only
→ I understand	yes, but…
→ opportunity	problem
→ challenging	difficult
→ motivated	stressed
→ interested	worried
→ possible	impossible
→ you, your	I, me, my
→ love	hate

Using positive words leads the way to a more generous and upbeat perspective. Your graciousness will become a beautiful foundation for good manners.

Tips for Great Conversations

→ Less is better—no need to tell all.

→ Be a good listener. People love to be around sympathetic listeners.

→ Good conversation requires give and take. Do both.

→ Think before you speak.

→ Be tactful and appropriate. You don't need to talk about your last surgery.

→ Stay light and maintain a good sense of humor.

→ Stay away from sarcasm and malice.

→ Don't try to be clever. Just be real.

→ Avoid talking about you. "Me…me…me" is really boring.

→ Try to find a topic on common ground.

→ Silence is acceptable. You don't have to fill "dead air" time.

→ Be sure to ask the other person to share something.

→ Don't monopolize one person—mingle.

→ Be polite when you excuse yourself from a conversation.

Moving a Conversation Along

Be aware of the amount of time you're talking to someone at a party or business meeting. Be sensitive not to spend too much time with one person—even if you're having a good conversation. There are several polite ways to make a break.

The first subtle indicator is to change your body language. Break eye contact briefly. Then touch the person lightly on the arm, offer a cordial handshake or hug (whatever is appropriate), or give a slight nod and use a kind phrase, such as:

→ "It's been nice talking to you."

→ "I've really enjoyed catching up with you and your family."

→ "I'm so glad you came. Have you met Karen? Karen, this is Jim."

→ "Gardening is so interesting. I hope we can get together soon to talk about it more."

→ "Excuse me. I need to go take care of something."

Whatever you do, don't start a new topic of discussion.

Giving and Receiving Compliments

*C*ompliments help people feel good about themselves. Be genuine when communicating praise or words of encouragement. Don't flatter someone or say something you don't mean. And don't go overboard. Excessive compliments waters them down.

Compliments should never be given with the expectation that the recipient will return the favor. Sometimes people want a compliment in return. If they tell people they like their outfits, they hope the people will say the same about theirs. So release that expectation and enjoy a pure moment of giving to someone. People love receiving compliments, but so often they are few and far between!

Along with giving compliments, we also need to receive them graciously. The best thing to do is smile and say, "Thank you!" If you feel shy and awkward about the compliment, avoid responding with something negative, such as, "This dress is not a good look for me. It's so out of style" or "Not really, but you're nice to say that." That essentially tells the compliment giver he or she is a liar or has poor perception. A negative response also might force the compliment giver to try to convince you the compliment was sincere and real. Then you both are feeling awkward and uncomfortable. So it's best to be grateful for the kind words and accept them with grace.

Active Listening

When you're talking to someone, listen at least as much as you talk. In other words you should be talking half the time or less. People love good listeners! Here are four ideas to help you become one.

> → *Listen attentively.* Don't tune in to another conversation in the room. In the same vein, don't let your mind wander to what you're going to say or what project you're going to work on tomorrow. One of the greatest gifts we can offer someone is our undivided attention.

> → *Keep good eye contact.* Look directly at the other person (but don't stare) as you listen and talk.

> → *Use body language as encouragement.* Smile and nod your head occasionally so the talker knows you're listening.

→ *Interrupt rarely.* Let the other person finish
before you respond or change the subject.

If the person you're talking to is shy, help out by
asking questions. Use open-ended queries that require
more than a simple yes or no. For instance, "Tell me
what you like about your job" or "What do you do for
fun?" These comments provide a loose structure that
may help the person share.

Most people love to talk about their lives. Sincere
and polite questions will help you learn a lot about your
new friend and vice versa as you share about your life.
And if there is a momentary lull in the conversation,
don't feel obligated to talk just to fill the silence. Mind-
less chatter is seldom interesting.

Good Conversation Don'ts

*T*hink of good conversation as a work of art. You
have an opportunity to be unique, creative, interesting, and garner the interest of another person. As
mentioned, the key to a great conversation is a two-to-
one ratio. Listen twice as much as you talk. Communicating involves carefully listening to the other person
until he or she is finished, responding appropriately, and

sharing your thoughts on the subject. Manners or guidelines exist to help make every person feel comfortable. So in a social conversation, avoid:

+ confessing
+ debating
+ gossiping
+ insulting
+ interviewing

+ notifying
+ scolding
+ shouting
+ talking over others
+ telling what to do

Get the most out of your voice, facial expressions, and body language. Your smile, your humor, and your posture can impact how you come across.

Social Graces

Introductions

*T*he first rule is that the person who is highest in authority is mentioned first. For instance, you would say the name of the president before the name of the janitor. If position isn't an issue, the oldest person's name is mentioned first. "Mom, I'd like you to meet the teenager who mows my lawn." If the ages are similar or not important, the woman's name is mentioned first. "Donna, I'd like you to meet Jim." This means you would say:

- ✤ Mayor Robertson, this is Nancy who lives on State Street.

- ✤ Dad, this is my swimming partner, Jan.

- ✤ Mary, this is Dan.

When introducing people, it's always nice to add a personal detail that might help the new friends start a conversation. When introducing a man and a woman to someone, you could say, "Peggy and Chad Merrihew, I'd like to introduce Christine Ianni, my granddaughter." Then the new acquaintances should shake hands.

To introduce an older person to a child: "Mrs. Whitney, I'd like you to meet Dax Lindsey. Dax, this is my friend, Mrs. Whitney. She is my neighbor and owns a beautiful collie."

Be friendly and relaxed when making introductions. Say the names clearly, emphasizing the pronunciation if a name is unusual. In a group setting you might want to tell how you know the person: "Dax, Chad lives three doors down from us."

When Your Mind Goes Blank

At one time or another all of us will draw a blank when we see people and need to introduce them to another person. So what do you do? Be honest: "I know we've met before and I remember the occasion, but I can't remember your name." Or "Hi, I'm Emilie. We knew each other a long time ago." Or "We're both friends of Jenny's, but I don't remember your name." Or "I'm sorry, my mind is blank. I recognize your face, but will you remind me what your name is?"

Another option at a social gathering is to invite another friend into the conversation. Perhaps that person will casually reveal the person's name. For example,

if you brought your son into the social circle you could
say, "Let me introduce you to my son Brad." The person
whose name you can't remember will probably introduce him- or herself to Brad.

When You're Introduced

When you're being introduced to someone, ask the
person you're meeting to repeat his or her name if you
didn't hear it clearly or you didn't catch the pronunciation. If you meet someone you haven't seen for a
long time, help the person by giving your name: "Hello,
I'm Yoli Brogger. We met last year at the fundraiser for
Women of Vision." If someone approaches you in this
way, take a cue that the person may not remember your
name and reintroduce yourself as well.

If someone comes up and says his or her name to
you, this is your cue to return the favor. For example, at
a school's open house a mother might say, "Hello, I'm
Barbara, David's mother." That's your cue to say, "It's so
nice to meet you. I'm Donna, Anissa's mom."

A Confident Handshake

A firm handshake communicates confidence, good
will, interest, and courtesy. The handshake has

lost some of its emphasis in casual contact, but it's still used in business and formal settings. Whether it's an accurate reflection or not, a limp handshake is often interpreted as saying the person is indecisive and weak willed. What's a proper handshake?

- → Hold your right hand out with your fingers together and your thumb raised.

- → Be firm in your grip—not too hard or not too soft. Keep your hand firm throughout the motion.

- → Don't make a face if the other person squeezes too hard, has a limp handshake, or feels clammy.

- → High-fives and knuckles are only for people you know well. Stick with the traditional handshake for most occasions.

- → When being introduced to a woman, wait until she offers her hand before you extend yours.

Practice shaking hands with someone or reach out to shake hands the next time you meet someone. Note how it feels and what you discern from the gesture. Hopefully it will help you start your conversation or meeting with more confidence.

When Something Embarrassing Happens

*W*e're human. That means there will be times when embarrassing situations occur. Let's review a few of the common ones and how you can respond.

→ *Yawning.* When a yawn is coming on, place your hand over your mouth and say, "Please excuse me. I'm enjoying our conversation, but I didn't get a good night's sleep last night."

→ *Rumbling stomach.* If you can ignore it, do so. However, if those around you can also hear your hunger pangs, say, "It must be close to lunch time—or at least my stomach thinks so."

→ *Hiccups.* Excuse yourself for a moment, go to the restroom or a private room, try some deep breathing, take a drink of water, and repeat as needed until they subside.

→ *Bad breath.* Use breath fresheners before you meet with others. If someone offers you a mint in a crowd, it might be a signal that your breath reflects the garlic you had last evening. Accept the mint and say thank you.

→ *Sneezing or coughing.* At the first sign of that tingle or tickle in your throat, cover your nose and mouth with a napkin, handkerchief, or the crook of your arm to prevent germs getting on your hands and spreading to those around you. Turn your head away from the crowd or away from food. After sneezing say, "Please excuse me." Wash your hands or use hand sanitizer as soon as possible.

→ *Accidents at the table.* It's embarrassing to knock over a beverage or spill food from a serving dish, but we all do it at some point. Use a napkin to mop up the table until the waiter or the person next to you offers to help. If at a good friend's home, you can jump up and grab some paper towels or a dishcloth to absorb the spillage. If the food or liquid gets on the floor, immediately notify your host so the carpet or flooring won't get stained. After the incident, apologize and move on. Don't keep apologizing. Keep the disruption as low-key as possible.

Those Awkward Moments

*H*ave you experienced moments when you're not sure how you're supposed to respond or react? We've all had them. Here are a few tips:

→ *To hug or not to hug.* If the person is a relative or close friend, it's perfectly okay to gently hug. If you're being introduced for the first time, hold off on the hug unless the other person indicates one is acceptable. Otherwise extend your hand for a shake and say, "Hello! I'm glad to meet you." For women, if you're meeting a business colleague or client with whom there is genuine friendship, then it's okay to greet with a light and quick hug.

→ *Let's have lunch together.* Don't offer this suggestion if you don't mean it. If you do mean it, be sure to follow up in a few days and get the lunch date on your calendar.

→ *Watch your language.* Be sensitive to those around you. Don't be disrespectful to people by using improper language. Off-color jokes and four-letter words are never appropriate.

→ *Be on time.* Being late shows disrespect for the

people waiting. When you're late because you didn't manage your time well, you're essentially telling people your time or your goals are more important than theirs. If being late is unavoidable, contact the people waiting for you as soon as possible, explain the situation, and offer to reschedule or give your estimated time of arrival.

The hardest job kids face today is learning good manners without seeing any.

FRED ASTAIRE

At the Table

What to Expect at a Formal Dinner

The number of courses offered and the food choices will depend on how formal the dinner is and the host's budget. The usual offering is five courses:

1. *Appetizers or hors d'oeuvres*. For informal events, these can be as simple as nuts, cheese, and crackers in serving dishes placed around the room or on a buffet for socializing before the meal. More formal dinners will serve an appetizer at the table as soon as everyone has found their seats.

2. *Soup* usually follows the appetizers.

3. *Salad*. A small salad is next.

4. The *main entrée* will be meat, fish, pasta, or poultry, along with an offering of vegetables and a starchy food.

5. *Dessert and a hot beverage.* Top off the dining experience with a delicious dessert and good coffee or tea. Many people these days are health conscious and watching their calorie intake, so offering fruit slices and an assortment of cheeses are alternatives to a traditional dessert.

Napkin Basics

After being seated, watch the host. When he or she unfolds the napkin, that's the signal for you to do likewise. Following these general rules will make you a great guest:

→ Always use your napkin—even if you're at an informal gathering or BBQ.

→ Unfold the napkin to the half fold position and place it in your lap, with the centerfold toward your waistline.

→ If you have to leave the table during the meal, place your napkin on the seat of your chair. This indicates to the server that you'll be returning.

→ When you're finished with the meal, place

your napkin to the right of your plate. Don't refold the napkin, but place it neatly.

→ Blot your mouth with your napkin after drinking and eating to avoid crumbs or liquid droplets on your chin.

If you're going to be hosting a very formal gathering, consider offering black napkins. Any lint from light-colored linen napkins is very noticeable against dark clothing.

Quick Table Tips

*T*hese quick tips cover the basics. It's amazing how easy it is to forget or forego the little touches in etiquette. We let so many courtesies slide in our finger-food lifestyle. Casual is enjoyable, but manners still come into play when we're dining with others, even when it involves plastic forks!

→ When asked to pass the salt, pass the pepper too.

→ Avoid placing your elbows on the table.

→ Never hunch over your food or "hug" your plate.

→ When hosting, serve your guests first.

→ When eating family style, food is passed to the right (counterclockwise) to avoid awkward passing moments.

→ Don't waste food. Only take what you will eat.

→ Cutting your salad into bite-sized pieces is a personal choice. If the salad greens are in large pieces, cutting them will make the salad easier to eat.

→ Women, blot your lipstick before the meal. This avoids leaving difficult-to-remove stains on napkins and cups. After dinner, if you want to touch up your lipstick, excuse yourself and go somewhere private.

→ If you get lemon seeds, olive pits, and watermelon seeds in your mouth, do not spit them into your napkin. Unobtrusively spit them into your spoon or your hand and put the seeds on the side of your plate.

→ If food gets lodged between your teeth, excuse yourself from the table and take care of the problem in private.

Handling Special Foods Gracefully

$\mathcal{M}$ ost of us know how to eat basic foods properly, but what about the awkward-to-eat and unusual foods? Avoid embarrassment by following these tips.

→ *Artichokes.* Pull off a leaf, dip it into the sauce, put most of the leaf in your mouth, gently close your teeth, and then quietly yet firmly pull the leaf out. You're scraping off the edible bottom part of the leaf. Don't eat the tips. When all the leaves have been eaten, take a knife or fork and scrape or cut out the fuzzy center covering and seeds (sometimes called "the choke" because that's what happens if you eat that part). This reveals the heart, which is delicious. Place the leaf discards and center covering in the provided plate or bowl or on the side of your plate.

→ *Asparagus.* If this vegetable is served raw, pick up the stem with your fingers and eat it. If cooked or served with a sauce, cut it into bite-sized pieces and eat with a fork.

→ *Chicken.* Southerners usually consider fried chicken finger food, especially at picnics, beach parties, and informal meals. At formal dinners your poultry will be cooked with wines and sauces, so use a knife and fork.

→ *Corn on the cob.* At informal meals you can eat the corn holding the cob ends with your hands or using small corncob skewers. Another option is to shave the corn off the cob with a sharp knife. Eat the kernels with a fork.

→ *Dips.* Don't double dip. When dipping chips, crackers, or vegetables, you only get one dip into the "community" sauce or dressing. An alternative is to put some dip on your plate. Then you can dip to your heart's content. Dipping can be messy, so make sure your napkin is ready.

→ *Fish.* Fish is a great, healthy food, but watch out for the bones. If you're served a whole or half fish, gently fork the end of the spine and pull up gently but firmly. Most of the bones should come right out. However, unobtrusively check to make sure you didn't miss any. If you do get a bone in your mouth, remove it discreetly and place it on the side of your plate.

→ *Salads.* Salads come in two ways. The greens are torn into small pieces and mixed with bite-sized vegetables, making it easy to eat with a fork, or the greens are served in large pieces. Use a knife or the side of your fork to cut the large greens into bite-sized pieces.

→ *Shellfish.* When eating shellfish that have legs, pull off the legs and eat the meat by hand. The main shells can be cracked with a metal nutcracker or crushed with a mallet. Extract the meat with your fork or sharp little forks your host provides. With shrimp, you can use fingers if it's served in the shell. If it's been peeled, eat with a knife and fork. With oysters, muscles, and similar foods, when cooked they will pop slightly open. If served shell and all, use a knife to pry them open. Use a spoon or fork to pull out the meat. With shellfish, often melted butter or other sauces are provided for dipping.

→ *Soup.* When eating soup, fill the spoon with liquid by dipping it into the bowl and then scooping away from you. A handy reminder: "As the ships sail out to sea, I spoon my soup away from me." Often special spoons are provided: large oval spoons for clear soups, large round spoons for cream soups, small round spoons for broths, and porcelain spoons for Chinese soups. Japanese soup may be presented in a lacquer bowl, which is lifted to the mouth instead of using a spoon. Except for the Japanese bowl, never drink soup from the bowl. And never slurp. When finished, leave the spoon in the bowl or rest it on the soup plate.

→ *Spaghetti.* Contrary to popular myth, pasta is not to be twirled against a spoon—not even in Italy. It is twirled on the fork against the plate until it forms a tight ball that can be easily raised to your mouth. Make sure the sauce doesn't drip on your clothes. Feel free to ask for a bib or covering if you want to be extra careful about your clothes.

→ *Sushi and sashimi.* Lift sushi off the serving plate with chopsticks. You can use the chopsticks or your fingers to dip the sushi into the soy sauce mixture (usually includes green horseradish), and then eat it in one huge bite, if possible. In restaurants, sushi is served atop wasabi, a root-based complement to the sushi. Do not dip the wasabi into the soy sauce mixture. Ginger is often served with the sushi as a palate cleanser. Eat it between bites or between different types of sushi. Sashimi (the non-sushi food) is eaten with chopsticks or a fork.

Giving Thanks

Starting a meal with a prayer of thanks or a toast is a great way to bring everyone together. Here are three short prayers you can say or use as inspiration.

To God who gives us daily bread
A thankful song we raise
And pray that He who sends us food
Will fill our hearts with praise. Amen.

As we now from our bounty eat,
Keep us humble, kind, and sweet,
May we serve Thee, Lord, each day
And feel Thy love, dear Lord, we pray.

Come, dear Lord,
Be our guest and
Become our host,
Be pleased to
Bless this food and
Us who dwell here. Amen.

Does anyone want to live a life
that is long and prosperous?
Then keep your tongue from speaking evil
and your lips from telling lies!
Turn away from evil and do good.
Search for peace, and work to
maintain it.

PSALM 34

Dining Out

Hosting at a Restaurant

→ When inviting people to a meal at a restaurant, be very specific about date, time, and place.

→ The person doing the inviting is responsible for paying the bill unless previous arrangements are made. Make sure the payment arrangement is clear before going to the restaurant to avoid haggling over who is paying for what.

→ Ask your guests if they have any special dietary needs and if they have a favorite type of food. Select a restaurant close to their home or business and make the reservation.

→ Call your guest the afternoon before or the morning of the date to reconfirm the plans.

→ Arrive at the restaurant a few minutes before the appointed time. Check the table you've been assigned to make sure it's acceptable.

→ Give your guests the best seats. If there's a large window and beautiful scenery, give them the view.

→ If you're familiar with the restaurant, offer to make meal recommendations. If all of you are new to the location, ask the waiter for his or her recommendations.

→ If your guests are served first, encourage them to begin eating while their food is hot. If your order arrives first, wait until your guests are served before you begin eating.

→ If your get-together is social, conversation can be casual throughout the meal. If the coming together is for business, limit casual talk to 15 minutes and then get down to business.

Possible Hosting Issues

→ Be alert to your guests' facial and body language when they're eating. If something seems off, ask, "Is there anything wrong?" or "Would you like me to call the waiter over?" Some guests might be bashful about wanting something changed, such as having their entrée cooked a little longer. However, if your guest answers, "No, no problem," take his or her word for it.

❖ If you're having a problem with the service or food, excuse yourself and go up front to talk to the waiter or manager. Don't get your guest involved in a dispute or confrontation (even if it's minor). In some cases you may want to wait until you get home or back to your office and call the restaurant manager.

❖ Bringing a business meal to a close can be awkward. After you've dined and discussed your business and set up any needed future meetings, stand up to signal the meeting is over. Thank the people for coming and walk to the door together. If you didn't pay the bill at the table, say goodbye again at the door and then walk to the register line as your guests leave.

When You're the Guest

When dining at a restaurant as a guest, there are some very good principles to observe:

❖ *Be on time.* If you're going to be late for any reason, call your host or, if the meeting is supposed to begin right now, call the restaurant as soon as possible to get the information to your host.

→ If you arrive before your host, wait patiently. If the maître d' offers to seat you, go ahead but leave the names of the people you're meeting with the front counter person. When seated, don't order anything or unfold your napkin until the other people arrive.

→ If you arrive late and other guests have already been served the first course, begin at the same point they are so your meal progression isn't out of sync.

→ When selecting from the menu, wait for the host to order and use that as a general price range gauge. If the host states you may order whatever you wish, feel free to do so but be reasonable.

→ Let the host deal with the waiter, especially in a business meeting.

→ If this is a business meeting, let your host bring the conversation around to the business topic.

→ Never arm wrestle to pay the check. Your host will take care of the bill unless other arrangements have been made in advance.

→ Send a thank-you note to the host within three days.

❖

Restaurant Dining

→ Women should never apply makeup at the table.

→ Be considerate. Keep conversations quiet and appropriate.

→ Turn your cell phone off during the meal. If you need to be on call, let people know when you sit down. If your phone rings, go to a convenient place to talk where you won't disturb anyone's meal or conversation. Keep the conversation short.

→ Pace your eating so the rest of the party and you will finish eating close to the same time.

→ Avoid piling papers and notes on the table. It makes it hard for the waiter to know where to place food items.

→ If your party or you take extra time to finish the meal and visit, consider giving the waiter an extra tip.

→ Don't table hop. If you make eye contact with someone you know, nod your head in acknowledgment but stay with your party. On

your way out after the meal, you can briefly
stop by and say hello, but don't linger.

→ Don't use your napkin as a handkerchief. If
you have a coughing or sneezing fit, excuse
yourself from the table until you have it under
control.

→ If you start choking and leave the table, don't
leave alone. Gesture for someone to accom-
pany you in case you need medical assistance.

The Art of Silverware

*M*ost of the time dealing with silverware is pretty
straightforward. We get a spoon, knife, and fork.
And sometimes it doesn't even matter which utensil
we decide to use. But when it comes to formal dining,
people can get confused about what to use and when.
Surprisingly, a formal dinner setting isn't as hard to figure out as it looks.

The main principle is that you start from the outside
utensils and work in toward the plate during the meal.
As talked about earlier, formal dinners usually have five
courses in this order: appetizers or hors d'oeuvres, soup,
salad, main entrée, and dessert with beverage.

Following this general guideline, each place setting would include a salad fork, dinner fork, and dessert fork. The first two forks go on the left side of the plate. Since salad is the first course eaten at the table, it goes on the far left. The main entrée is next, so the dinner fork is next to the plate. The dessert fork is special, so it sits on the table above the plate, tines pointed to the right.

Spoons and knives go on the right side of each plate. Again, you start on the outside and work in during the meal. So the first spoon you use is the one on the outside, which would be the soup spoon. Next would be the teaspoon. The dinner knife is next to the plate, sharp side pointed toward the plate.

I know this can be confusing. See page 62 for a clear presentation of a formal place setting.

Did you know that silverware also helps you communicate with the server? The placement of your utensils lets the server know what stage of the meal is being served and whether you're finished with that course. If you've just paused eating for a breather, place the utensils in the resting position (fork and knife crossing at the center of the plate with handles resting on opposite sides).

When you're done with your meal, place your utensils at the four o'clock position, handles facing out. This lets your server know your plate can be removed.

A. napkin

B. service plate

C. soup bowl on a liner plate

D. bread and butter plate with butter knife

E. water glass

F. red wine glass

G. white wine glass

H. salad fork

I. dinner fork

J. dessert fork

K. knife

L. teaspoon

M. soup spoon

Resting Position

Finished Position

Tipping Guidelines

→ When dining out, the typical tip is 15 to 18 percent. For parties of six or more, many restaurants add an 18-percent gratuity to the bill. If you receive poor service, talk to the manager about decreasing the gratuity.

→ Tip a coat attendant one to two dollars.

→ Tip a valet who parks your car one to two dollars. Tip when you leave the car and when you pick it up. Tipping is not part of the charges posted for valet service.

→ Tip musicians, if present, one to two dollars. If several songs are played especially for you and your guests, consider five dollars.

→ Tip a restroom attendant 50 cents to a dollar. Often there is a "tip bowl" on the counter.

→ When eating at a cafeteria or buffet, no tipping is required. However, if a waiter brings you drinks and removes plates, consider leaving a 10-percent tip.

❧ Food servers on average make half their
income from gratuities. Often your tip is
pooled and distributed among restaurant
employees, including the maître d', people
clearing tables, and dishwashers.

Family Manners Matter

Mentoring Manners

Teaching manners through lessons and books works well, but the best way to lay a solid foundation for being considerate of others is to model how to treat others and what being polite is all about. Children pick up early how to deal with others by watching parents, teachers, and other adults. It's never too late to model good manners.

→ *Show empathy.* To empathize is to understand how others feel, to walk in their shoes. Talk with your kids and others about how people might feel in easy and difficult situations. Discuss emotions with them, explaining what they are and that they are good indicators of what's happening with them and around them. At a very young age a child can identify emotional feelings, such as happy, glad, angry, bored, sad, and scared. Praise your kids when you see them relate to people or even pets in an empathetic manner.

→ *Encourage children (and adults) to see how people of different backgrounds act, speak, and live.* People from different cultures, religions, and value systems may respond differently than we do. Take time to talk about these differences, noting how differences aren't right or wrong, just new ways to look at events and situations. This also gives you an opportunity to talk about how to evaluate behavior to ascertain whether something is right or wrong, good or bad.

→ *Praise children when they show good manners.* Continually be on the lookout for opportunities to praise children for good behavior. Positive reinforcement encourages repeats of the good behavior.

→ *Be concerned about others.* Show genuine concern and care for the basic needs of others. Children will model your behavior, so how they respond and interact with others in their later years is greatly affected by what you're doing with them today. Encourage community participation and support. Let them volunteer. Animal shelters need people to pet, love, and help socialize the animals, and many

charitable organizations have places where
children and adults can help.

→ *Practice what you preach*. Children will see
through you if your walk is different than your
talk. They notice how people respond to various conflicts. How do you react to the police
when you're pulled over for a traffic violation?
How do you treat someone on the street corner who asks for money? Do you forgive those
who offend you? Is your voice level consistent
with a calm approach when you get upset? Do
you apologize when you're wrong?

When you're around adults and children, you have a
tremendous opportunity to show your values by example and to model your faith. What you do can positively
impact today, tomorrow, and the future.

Encouraging a Supportive Family

*E*ach family is unique. Some members are functional
and some may be dysfunctional, but they are all
family. Family can be the most effective and consistent
support for each member. How can you encourage and
nurture a supportive environment?

→ As a family, celebrate as many special occasions as possible, including birthdays, anniversaries, holidays, and religious celebrations. Teach your children to consider or notice what others might like or need. And don't forget that some of the best gifts aren't purchased and don't have to be expensive. Consider giving "get out of a chore" coupons, spending time doing something special, going on family hikes, and so forth.

→ When something of importance in the family occurs (a brother gets a promotion, a nephew makes the basketball team, a niece plays first chair in the orchestra, a daughter wins a contest, a husband gets a promotion), do something to honor that person. And make sure your kids know about it and participate. Don't just sit back and say, "Wouldn't it be nice to send a card with a check inside." Do it!

→ Establish a "you are special" plate for special occasions. You can buy a "you are special" plate or pick a unique one to use. Remember to get it out for all special occasions…or even times when someone needs encouragement. When you do use it, have everyone present say something positive about the person being honored.

- Watch for times when a family member or neighbor needs help and take advantage of the opportunity. Does someone need help to get to an appointment, to pay bills, to get the lawn mowed, to have some shopping done? Or maybe someone needs to receive a plate of warm cookies to cheer up the day? Actively seek ways to help, and get your kids and other family members involved.

- Keep family members up-to-date on family news. Promote sharing within the family and model how to make the family a supportive and safe environment for honesty and being real.

- Be sensitive to family members. Someone may need help with finances, children, job stresses, and relationships. Look for ways to show you care and find ways to help.

- Attend events and activities to show your love and support. Go to family-member-related open houses, athletic events, church performances, and other activities. Write notes of encouragement and recognize involvement during mealtimes.

- Invite singles, including widows and widowers, to family gatherings. We live in a couples'

world, and singles often feel left out and iso-
lated.

→ Plan regular family get-togethers. Coordinate
gatherings, help out at family reunions, and
encourage family togetherness. Remember to
offer to contribute financially for incidentals if
someone is hosting a gathering.

→ Send greeting cards to relatives in honor of
birthdays, anniversaries, engagements, weddings, and so forth. Send cards to say "I hope
you feel better," "Just a note to say I'm thinking of you," and "I'm sorry for your loss."

→ Keep a journal listing relatives and details
about them that can be passed down through
the family. Become the family historian and
share often the interesting details and backgrounds of your family line.

✤

When Someone Is in the Hospital

*M*any people feel awkward and aren't sure what
to do when a loved one or friend is sick and/
or in the hospital. With a little advance thought about

how to respond to such occurrences, we can handle these times with grace, sensitivity, and kindness. We can also be a support for the patient and for their family members and friends as they cope with the anxiety such times produce.

> ❖ Cheer up the sick or recovering person with a telephone call every other day or so. Always ask if it's a good time for the person to talk and respond accordingly. Keep the message uplifting and short. Remember to say "I love you." If the hospital room doesn't have a telephone by the bed, leave a message at the nurses' station. Someone will deliver it for you. Some hospitals have online message centers you can use.

> ❖ Ask if the ailing person wants visitors before showing up. Once there, be sensitive to the person's energy level.

> ❖ Ask if the patient is as comfortable as possible. For example, if your loved one or friend is cold, offer to find a nurse and see if you can arrange another blanket.

> ❖ Ask if there is anything you can do—babysit the children, bring a meal or snack, go to the bank, do something for them at home, bring books or magazines.

➔ Take some photos of family and friends to the hospital room so the sick person will be reminded that he or she is loved.

➔ Replace wilted flowers with fresh ones. Help keep the room neat and cheery.

➔ When taking or sending flowers or gifts, keep them small if the patient will need to haul them home.

➔ If something medical happens to the person while you're visiting, remain calm, keep a supportive look on your face, and stay out of the way of the attending nurses.

➔ Ask if the person would like prayer for anything specific. Follow through by praying with him or her right away.

When to Bring the Kids Along

There are plenty of places you can take your children that are appropriate. Here are considerations if you have young children:

➔ *Don't assume that children are invited to*

functions. If the invitation doesn't specifically
include children, don't take them.

→ *Unless you're very good friends, don't ask your
host if you can bring your children to an event.*
This would put your host in an awkward position. If you're not comfortable being away
from your children or you don't have someone to care for your children, don't accept
the invitation. When you decline the invitation, you can mention the reason, but don't
expect the host to accommodate you by inviting your kids.

→ *Be thoughtful when visiting friends without children.* Not every home is child-friendly. When
you're making a short visit to chat or to drop
something off, be sensitive and keep track of
your children.

→ *Take along toys or reading material* to keep your
children occupied while you visit.

→ *Don't let your kids run wild.* Keep them from
running around, yelling, handling knick-
knacks, and interrupting when you're visiting someone. Teach them to stand next to you
and wait to be recognized if they want to share
something with you while you're visiting.

Children in Public

*I*t's up to you to make sure each outing is a positive learning experience for your child, comfortable for you, and not an imposition on others.

→ *At restaurants.* If the restaurant you're planning to go to is not equipped for children, go to a different one. Nothing is worse than taking a young child to a fine restaurant and ruining the quiet, festive occasion for other guests. If you are at a restaurant and one of your children starts crying or throwing a tantrum, quickly take the child outside or to someplace where they won't disturb other diners. Although you may be used to a child crying and fussing, some diners won't be.

→ *Church functions.* Most churches provide wonderful nursery facilities for your children, but if they don't have childcare, carefully consider the risk of disturbing others during services. If your church has a "cry room," this is great to use when the children are young. If nothing is provided for the kids, sit in the back and immediately take your child out of the service and to a quiet place if they start making a fuss or are being noisy.

→ *Entertainment events.* Whether the event is indoors or outdoors, the audience is there to be entertained by someone other than your children. If you have no alternative but to bring your child, sit in an area where you can exit if the need arises. Often parents try to calm their children back into quiet mode, but those few minutes of fussing can be really frustrating for people trying to listen and take in the event.

You can get through life with bad manners, but it's easier with good manners.

LILLIAN GISH

Let us not become weary in doing good, for at the proper time we will reap a harvest if we do not give up. Therefore, as we have opportunity, let us do good to all people, especially to those who belong to the family of believers.

APOSTLE PAUL

Relationships and Manners

Making a True Friend

*O*ne of the best ways to make that new person a solid friend is to invite him or her to a meal. You can prepare it yourself or go to a restaurant or luncheon function. If that goes well, do it again and try other situations.

→ If you think your new friend would feel more comfortable with others around, invite a few people to join you.

→ Don't always be the invitee. It's important that you be a giver too. And it doesn't always have to be in like fashion. Instead of another meal, invite your friend to a sporting event, a play, or a community service activity.

→ Remember not to gossip or share personal information about your friend with others. Protect your friends if someone else wants to gossip or share about them by coming to your friend's defense if necessary or changing the subject.

→ Good friends stay in touch even when busy.

Often you have to be flexible to fit in activities that might not always be more convenient to your calendar. Be willing to accommodate your friend's schedule. Almost everyone is busy these days so don't let that excuse keep you from making your friend a priority.

→ The best friends are your "two in the morning" friends. They are available in an emergency. Make sure you're available to them as well. Be willing to babysit on a last-minute notice, pick up your friend's children from school, run an errand when needed, help friends move or do projects. Be willing to do the unexpected.

→ When your friend is having difficulties and/or is struggling, give him or her some slack. Be willing to help and be willing to listen.

→ Be willing to try something new, do something different, or attend a function you might not normally do. Broaden your horizons and do something someone else wants to do to spend time together.

Meeting People

*H*ave you ever wished for a stronger circle of friends or a best friend? Developing friendships requires being willing to open yourself up to new experiences and venues. When you adorn yourself with good manners and a kind heart, you'll find it easy to make friends in many situations. Here are some tips for getting connected.

- ✦ Don't turn down an invitation to a party or event. A new friend might be there. Be willing to try something unusual or out of your comfort zone.

- ✦ Blind dates may be scary, but that person may turn out to be someone really special to you. And perhaps he or she will know some exciting people you'll enjoy meeting.

- ✦ Be open to joining groups that specialize in your interests, such as ski clubs, book clubs, chess clubs, hiking associations, community service organizations, and theater groups.

- ✦ Churches and nonprofit organizations are always looking for volunteers. This type of meeting place can be uplifting because you're giving of yourself. Look for opportunities where you can give rather than take.

→ Become a volunteer at a hospital, a visitor for an elderly person in a nursing home who doesn't have family nearby, or help children in an elementary school work on their reading and math comprehension. Check with the institutions for opportunities and people who need help.

→ Cultural activities are a great place to be involved either as a season ticket holder, a one-performance ticket buyer, or as an usher or worker. Chance meetings happen at intermissions. You get to mingle with others, conversations start, and business cards and telephone numbers can be exchanged.

→ Associate with likeminded people at sporting events. Improve your tennis, golf, snow skiing, or waterskiing skills to the point where others will include you or invite you to be a partner. Others will see your skills and want to include you. After the session or game, see if anyone wants to go out for a bite to eat. And say yes if someone invites you.

→ Helping at your children's school is always a

great way to meet other people who are in the same life place you are and care about children.

→ Keep your eyes open. Pay attention to the people in your neighborhood. See if you can help out. Look for opportunities to do things in groups.

→ Take an education or community class to meet people and discover new areas of interest. Go to the related social functions and make the effort to engage in conversation with the other participants.

What Good Friends Do

What makes a good friend? Sometimes the simplest answer is the most profound: You like the person. You feel better when he or she is around. You feel refreshed when you're together. Good friends...

→ know friendships take time and effort. They're willing to make compromises for the friendship. Things don't always have to go one way—that person's way.

→ plan surprises, such as birthday parties, secret gifts, impromptu movies, quick cups of coffee.

→ handle drop-by visits graciously. They don't worry that their homes aren't perfect. They greet you cheerfully.

→ give small gifts for no reason except the pleasure of seeing the joy on a friend's face.

→ fill in at the last minute to help with a carpool, offer a vacation home for the weekend, or help plan a birthday party for a son or daughter.

Some friendships are as comforting and comfortable as a well-worn pair of shoes. Others are full of excitement and adventure. The best ones are filled with laughter, softened with tears, and strengthened with a spiritual bond.

When You're Dating...or Want To

→ Give the person a call at least three days before your desired date time.

→ Make your first date one that matches the other person's interests. Consider a movie, a baseball game, a hike, or a bike ride.

→ Avoid changing plans at the last minute.

→ Be on time.

→ Dress for the occasion. Make a good impression.

→ Be sensitive to budgets. Tradition says the man pays for the date. If stepping outside this tradition, discuss it beforehand. Some people may be uncomfortable not being in charge, and sometimes women may feel obligated if men always pay.

→ Keep the conversation upbeat and clean.

→ If you don't feel well or are tired, present a positive attitude anyway.

→ Look for opportunities to laugh and have fun. Remember to take your sense of humor along.

→ If you don't know the person well, meet at the date location so you have your own transportation. Make sure the first few dates are in public places for safety reasons.

→ If the date is going in the wrong direction, make an excuse and go home early. If you're uncomfortable with your date's talk, behavior, or attitude, take the necessary steps to be safe and leave the situation, whether that means calling a cab, asking a restaurant manager to help you, or calling the police if the situation becomes difficult. Trust your instincts.

→ At the end of the evening say thank you for the evening even if the chemistry wasn't that great between the two of you.

→ If the person wants to see you again and you would like to have another date, say yes. If you weren't on the same wavelength, be up-front and say, "Thank you for tonight, but I'm not interested in a dating relationship right now." It's okay to be firm and frank. Be courteous, but direct.

Respect for ourselves guides our morals;
respect for others guides our manners.

LAURENCE STERNE

Daily Courtesies

Going Shopping

→ If you have children, remember to keep them under control.

→ If you see food items knocked off the shelf or on the floor, pick them up and put them back in the proper position on the shelf or put them in your cart and take them to the cashier.

→ Watch for traffic when you turn and stop abruptly.

→ Be sensitive when you're checking out with a full basket of groceries. If the person behind you only has one or two items, consider letting him or her go through first.

→ Use the quick checkout register only when you meet the restrictions (10 to 12 items only).

→ Be friendly to the checkout personnel.

→ If someone assists you with your bags to the parking lot, tell him or her thank you.

→ Be environmentally sound. Take your own cloth or reusable bags for groceries. If you do get paper or plastic bags, recycle them.

→ Take your shopping cart to the proper storage location in the parking lot when you're done. If you see another cart in a parking space, why not take it to the storage place too?

⚜

Movie Manners

→ Be early or on time so that you don't have to crawl over or bump people to get to a seat.

→ Silence is a virtue once the movie has started. The sound of someone chewing popcorn, cracking gum, and rattling candy wrappers can be very annoying and mask the film's dialog. Don't let your behavior disturb those around you.

→ If you have to get up during the performance, exit with a minimum of distraction. Whisper "excuse me" as you step around people. If you know ahead of time you might have to leave early, arrive early so you can get a seat on the aisle.

→ When entering a filled row, face the people as you maneuver past them. They would rather see your face than your rear. Also remember to say "excuse me." If you step on someone's foot, say, "I'm sorry."

→ Leave the area around you clean. Don't assume that because it's a movie theater it's all right to throw junk on the floor. Take your beverage cup, candy wrappers, and empty popcorn boxes to the trash can at the movie room's entrance. It's the polite thing to do, and it makes less work for the cleanup crew. Teach your kids this kind of consideration too.

Interacting with Professionals

When dealing with professionals, whether they be doctors, dentists, lawyers, financial advisors, police, and so forth, if you treat them with respect, they will give you better service.

→ Respect who they are and their expertise.

→ Even though you pay for their services, let them know you appreciate all they do to help you.

→ Make the encounter a win-win experience. Approach the meetings or appointments with as upbeat an attitude as possible. You'll get better help, and they'll get a good client.

→ A thank-you note is appropriate if the person has done something exceptional or helped you significantly.

→ Be on time for appointments. Time is money for both of you.

→ Don't take advantage of professionals who are also your friends. If they perform a service for you, be sure to make payment at the going rate.

→ Don't corner professionals at social functions and ask for free advice. If you need information, call and set up an appointment.

Working with Repair People

*E*veryone wants and needs to be treated with dignity and respect. Make sure you treat the people you hire with courtesy and consideration.

→ Don't talk down to anyone or be condescending. Welcome workers with a friendly hello when they arrive.

→ Shake hands during introductions and refer to the person by name from that point on. First names go a long way in easing communication and establishing friendly rapport. If the repair person has an assistant, acknowledge him or her also.

→ Be specific and clear in stating what and where your problem is. Show the person what you're talking about. If communication isn't your strong suit, write down the problem as briefly as possible and the solution you're working for. If you want to be called if the repair will be more than a specific monetary amount, note that too.

→ Put the workers at ease when they arrive. If the work takes more than a few hours, offer something to drink occasionally.

→ When the repair is complete, inspect the work carefully and make sure you're satisfied before the service person leaves.

→ When you're satisfied with the work, say thank you and express your appreciation.

→ If you're really pleased with the work, send a note of appreciation to the company. Include the repair people's names, the date they did the work, the type of job, and the ways they excelled.

→ When you receive good service, recommend the service to your friends and neighbors to support that business and help the people you know.

Tipping

Tipping is a gesture of appreciation for good service. Don't be too frugal, but also don't overtip when the service doesn't justify it. Find a balance. And if a tip or gratuity is included in the bill and the service doesn't warrant it, talk to the manager about reducing the tip amount.

→ Hairdressers: 15 percent (if the stylist is the business owner, a tip isn't necessary)

→ Manicurists: $2

→ Masseuse: 10 to 20 percent

→ Bellhop: $2 for the first bag and $1 for each additional bag

✦ Tour guides: 15 to 20 percent of the ticket price

✦ Parking valet: $1 to $5 when you leave your car and again when you pick it up

✦ Doorman: $1 if he or she hails a cab or does another service for you

✦ Concierge: For good sporting event or concert tickets, tip $5 to $10

✦ Housekeeping staff: Leave a small tip in an envelope each morning instead of a larger amount at checkout because different workers may attend to the room during the week. This also may result in better service throughout your stay.

✦ Taxis: Depending on the trip length, tip $2 for short trips and 15 to 20 percent of the fare for longer trips. You can add $1 per bag if the service was good.

✦ During the Christmas holidays you might consider tipping your service people, such as paper deliverers, housecleaning personnel, and gardeners. Mail carriers can't accept cash, but they can accept gifts up to $20 in value.

Remember, we all like to feel appreciated. The amount of tip depends on your budget and how much you value the service.

Money and Materials

→ *Lending and borrowing items:* If an item hasn't been returned, it's okay to ask the borrower to return it. And when you borrow something, make sure you return it promptly and in good condition.

→ *Keep track of lending.* When lending, make a note of who borrowed it, when, and the expected time it will be returned. Make sure the person borrowing the item and you agree to the terms.

→ *Receiving an unusable gift:* If you receive a gift in the wrong size, style, or color, be sensitive in approaching the subject. First, say thank you for the person's thoughtfulness. Next explain your dilemma and share what you would like to do to correct the situation. In most cases the giver will understand and agree with you.

→ *Receiving an unwanted gift:* First, tell the giver thank you for thinking of you and sending a gift. After a reasonable period of time, you can regift the item, sell it, or donate it.

→ *Money:* Asking for money as a gift is inappropriate. If you do receive money, make sure

you respond with a thank-you note. As a
giver, money is almost always appreciated. As
a grandparent, I often give money when I'm
not sure what a grandchild might like. I'm
not always up on the latest fashion and tech
gadgets.

→ *Exchanging gifts with friends of means:* Gift-
giving is not a contest. Give only what you
can afford. Remember, nonmaterial gifts
make wonderful presents. Gift certificates for
a home-cooked dinner, for specific jobs done,
for services to be given, or for a dozen homemade cookies are wonderful to receive.

→ *Charging error:* Being a good consumer
requires checking bills for accuracy. If you've
been overcharged, quietly speak to the person responsible for your bill. If there's an error,
it will be corrected, and it becomes a learning
experience for you and the store. If you were
undercharged, point out the error and pay
what you owe.

*I have a respect for manners as
such. They are a way of dealing with
people you don't agree with or like.*

MARGARET MEAD

Quality Communication

Phone Talk

→ *Preparing to make a call.* The way you sit or stand affects your tone of voice. If you slump, your lungs can't fill completely with air so your voice won't sound strong and clear. When you sit up, your voice will sound positive and energized. Have any information you'll need for the call ready, and always have a pad and pen next to the phone for taking messages.

→ *When to call.* Most calls should be placed between eight in the morning and ten at night on weekdays. On Saturdays, ten to ten is a good standard, and on Sundays noon to ten works well. If you're calling outside your time zone, use the time zone you're calling to as your guide.

→ *Call waiting.* Unless you're expecting a call, let the second call go into voice mail. If you decide to answer the second call, talk to the second caller just long enough to say you're on another call and will return that person's call shortly. Make sure you honor your word and call back.

→ *Returning calls.* Personal calls should be returned the same day or within a 24-hour time span. Business calls should be returned as soon as possible, even if it's to tell the caller you will call back when you find the information.

Voice Mail

→ If you're in the middle of a very important task and don't want to be interrupted, have your calls forwarded to voice mail. When you do check your voice mail, respond to the calls as soon as you can.

→ Make sure your voice mail message is upbeat and short.

→ When you're going to be gone or away from your desk for an extended time, update your voice mail message. Record when you will and will not be in the office. In a businesslike voice, ask the caller to leave a brief message that includes date and time of call, the purpose of the call, and a number where he or she can be reached. Also say you'll return calls as soon as possible.

→ For personal voice mail, don't let people who call know you're on vacation or out of town. Just say you're unavailable, ask callers to leave the pertinent information, and mention you will return calls as soon as you can.

Cell Phones and Text Messaging

While cell phones are a great convenience, they can also be a distraction and keep us from interacting with the people around us. Remember, we control cell phones, they don't control us.

Cell Phone Do's

→ Keep your cell phone charged in case of emergencies.

→ When in public, keep your phone conversations to a minimum. Find a private place to continue your call or tell the person you'll call back. People talking on cell phones seem to forget that the people around them can hear the personal messages being delivered and discussed. Some people may recognize from the conversation who you're talking to and the people you're referencing. Also, the people around you don't want to hear you talk to your aunt about her surgery or how well your child is being toilet trained.

→ Keep your voice low when you're talking on your cell phone out of courtesy for your caller and the people around you.

→ If you tell someone you'll have your cell on if they need to reach you, make sure you do.

→ Turn your cell phone off when in libraries, restaurants, concerts, movie theaters, and other quiet public places.

→ When possible, turn your cell phone to vibrate so the ring doesn't interrupt the people around you.

→ Teach your kids cell phone and text messaging etiquette.

→ Insist that when texting you or other adults, your kids use complete sentences, proper grammar, and check spelling. This is good training for the business world.

Cell Phone Don'ts

→ When visiting with people, put your cell phone on vibrate or turn it off. If you do need to answer the phone, move to a place that is quiet and private and keep the conversation brief. When you choose to talk to the person on your cell in the presence of others, you're telling the people you're with they're not very important.

→ Don't share personal details, issues, concerns, or worries when talking on a cell phone in public.

→ Don't check text messages or voice mail messages when you're with someone else unless the call/message relates to that person as well.

→ Don't talk loudly on cell phones in public.

→ Don't talk on your phone or headset device while at a customer-service counter or drive-thru at stores, banks, or fast-food restaurants. Besides being inconsiderate of the customer service employee, you might be holding up the people behind you.

→ Don't use your cell phone conversation as a way to promote your business, personal importance, or to share information with the people around you. Be discreet.

❧ Turn off your cell phone when eating with family or friends.

❧ Do not text message at the table or when you're visiting with family or friends.

❧ Don't let your cell phone make you available 24 hours a day, 7 days a week. Everyone needs a break from being "on call."

❧ Avoid driving while talking on the phone. Many states have laws against this, and most of us have had to wait until cell phone talkers finally notice the light is green or traffic is clear at stop signs.

Written Correspondence

Handwritten correspondence is becoming a lost art, but business still depends on writing. The advent of e-mail has taught many people to take short-cuts in writing, which works well for personal communication but sends a poor message on a business level.

❧ *Proper greetings.* Start letters with the formal

salutations Mr., Mrs., and Ms. until you know someone in personal fashion.

→ *Handwritten.* Social notes should always be handwritten.

→ *Neatness.* Make sure your writing is legible and neat.

→ *Style and tone.* Your writing style can and should reflect your personality. If you're writing an informal note, you can be casual. In a more formal, business style, make sure your spelling, grammar, and word usage is accurate.

E-mail Etiquette

E-mails are great for what they are designed to do: communicate quick messages for business, personal use, and in some emergencies. But this medium does not work well when communicating heart to heart on something personal, handling complex subjects, or working through difficult issues. Words on a screen don't reflect the heart of the writer, and the reader can't see the facial expressions, gestures, and other nuances that reveal the intent of the words chosen.

→ *E-mail should always be professional.* Make sure your e-mail is written with good grammar, word choice, and clarity before hitting "send."

→ *Keep e-mails task oriented.* Company e-mails should only be used for company business.

→ *Make sure addressee in "to" box is correct.* With automatic name fill-in technology, your e-mail to "Mike" in your company's production department might accidentally go to a "Mike" who works at a different company.

→ *Remember, e-mails are not private correspondence.* E-mails written on company time, on company equipment, and sent to someone in your company or another company is your company's property. Many companies keep all e-mails in permanent archives.

→ *Be careful what you send.* Stories, jokes, and pictures can be entertaining and funny, but keep in mind who you are sending what to and where the person is. If someone sends you questionable material, ask them nicely to not send you material of that nature.

→ *Be cognizant of time.* Respect your time and the time of the people you're e-mailing. Keep anonymous stories and such to a minimum.

→ *E-mails can be permanent.* Your e-mail can be forwarded, saved, and printed by the person receiving it. This means people you don't know or never intended to get your message may receive it. Again, e-mail is not private correspondence.

Expressing Gratitude

*T*hink how much joy you feel when you receive a thank-you note. Pass that joy on to others by sending gratitude notes. You can send thanks...

→ when you receive a gift for any occasion

→ when you've been an overnight guest

→ when you've been a guest at a party

→ for kind acts extended to you

→ for being the guest of a friend or business associate at a meal

→ to express gratitude for flowers or donations on the death of a loved one

→ to a pastor for giving an inspirational sermon

→ to someone who sent you a get well card

> ⤳ to an employer for a bonus or raise
>
> ⤳ to someone who has done an exceptional job
>
> ⤳ to someone who help others

Never underestimate what a note means to another person.

What to Say

A note can be very brief in nature, but it should include several elements:

> ⤳ mention of the specific gift
>
> ⤳ an expression of its beauty or worth to you and how well it was presented
>
> ⤳ a mention of how you liked the gift and how you will use it
>
> ⤳ a positive, thoughtful closing remark, such as greetings to the family or a reiteration of how thoughtful they were
>
> ⤳ your signature

Don't use words or phrases that aren't normally in your vocabulary. Just be yourself—your grateful self—and let your heart shine.

Brushing Up on Business Manners

Business Manners Reflect Integrity

*G*ood manners are essential for business. Common sense (which isn't so common anymore) and consideration for others win respect and identify you as a team member who is a real asset to your company. Good manners also reflect a heart of integrity.

→ *Be consistent in how you treat people.* The low person on the totem pole should be treated with the same respect extended to the boss. Be nice to all people as you climb the ladder of success, and you will help build a better company.

→ *Exhibit loyalty to your boss and company.* Inside and outside your company, be loyal and aboveboard. Don't say anything about someone that you wouldn't say to that person directly. Extol the positives of your company.

Remember, the better your company does, the better you'll probably do.

→ *Hold off criticizing coworkers.* Unless you are a supervisor, criticizing coworkers is not part of your job. If you are a supervisor and must correct someone, do it face-to-face and in private. When possible, use the sandwich method: state a positive, state the negative and possible solutions, and state another positive.

→ *Be helpful to the new kid on the block.* The first few days have a lot of unknowns. Show the person around and introduce him or her to others in the department and company. Give them heads-up information about office procedures, breaks, and helpful information on supplies, work, and where to get help if needed.

→ *Stand by your word.* If you say you're going to do something, do it.

❧

Earn a Good Reputation

*Y*our reputation is your biggest asset…or your biggest hindrance. Protect your reputation and always work toward maintaining sterling character.

→ *Be punctual.* Don't be known as the one who keeps people waiting.

→ *Develop a sense of humor.* Humor sets the tone for a more casual and relaxed atmosphere. People like to be around people who can laugh. Humor can also defuse tense situations and provide respite during high pressure times.

→ *Be known as a giver.* If someone buys you lunch, the next time you buy lunch. Pull your weight.

→ *Be nice to everyone.* From the boss to the janitor, everyone works to make the business a success. Promote an "everyone is important and has value" atmosphere.

→ *Don't exaggerate your position.* Be humble. Don't brag about your position or accomplishments. It's better to "talk low and excel" than to "talk high and fail." Also few people succeed entirely on their own. A lot of people helped you get to where you are.

→ *Dress appropriately.* Be circumspect in how you dress for the office and social events affiliated with the company you work for. Let the company know you're proud to represent it so the owners will be proud that you are representing them.

→ *Be positive and sensitive.* Never put someone down or criticize someone in front of others.

→ *Give or share credit where it's due.* Don't take praise for something not of your doing and acknowledge any help you received.

→ *Promote teamwork.* Get in the habit of saying "we did this" or "we did that" instead of "I did this" or "I did that." Develop team spirit.

→ *Be responsible.* Admit when you make a mistake or when a project you were in charge of wasn't as successful as hoped.

Corporate Courtesies

→ *Respond to correspondence.* Acknowledge receipt of correspondence as soon as possible, preferably within five working days.

→ *Respond to all RSVPs promptly.* Respond within a week after receiving an invitation to a work-related event. Be sure to attend if you accept the invite.

→ *Keep borrowing from coworkers to a minimum.* Don't borrow from someone in the office if you aren't planning to return the item. When you do return it, make sure it's in the same or better condition than when you borrowed it.

→ *If someone is hospitable, return the favor.* A thoughtful thank-you note is always appreciated when someone does a favor for you or is helpful in some way.

→ *Be empathetic.* When a coworker receives bad news, listen attentively and compassionately.

→ *Share common information with your fellow workers.* No one likes to be left out of the loop. Collaboration is key to strong business relationships.

→ *Don't steal from your company.* That includes taking or "borrowing" stamps, pencils, computer time, telephone time, and taking long breaks.

→ *Practice making small talk with people.* The art of good communication is important for business and personal relationships. Good social skills are an asset in almost every occupation.

Show Respect

→ When a guest enters your office, stand, walk around your desk, and shake hands.

→ Always talk respectfully about your spouse and children.

→ A person who writes encouraging notes is remembered fondly and gets ahead in life.

→ Use your words to build people up. Be an encourager.

→ Thank the people who work hard to make your job possible. Put a note of appreciation in their personnel files.

→ Introduce people properly. For instance, always say the older person's name or the person with the highest authority first during introductions.

→ Use a firm handshake when you're introduced to someone or when you're saying goodbye.

→ When traveling with someone higher in the organization, give him or her the best seat in restaurants, taxis, and at events.

→ Keep silent when your boss is looking over business papers while traveling.

→ Make it your top priority to assist your boss in any way you can.

→ Being an assistant to your boss is a great opportunity to watch and learn. Many of today's CEOs started out as assistants. You'll also get plenty of opportunities to network with influential people.

Business Writing

→ Business letters should be typed, neat, clear, and direct. If you do need to handwrite a note, make sure your writing is legible.

→ Always include the addressee's name and full title in addition to the company name and address. The message and wording should be professional and respectful.

→ If your letter delivers bad news, be respectful and kind. You may need to deal with that person at another time or in a different capacity. Keep as many relationships positive as possible.

→ Express your thoughts clearly and briefly. Avoid clunky and dull language.

Business Phone Etiquette

Oftentimes the first experience a person has with your company is when they call. When answering the phone be respectful, pleasant, and willing to help. Greetings should include:

→ company name

→ name of person answering the phone

→ offer of help

For instance, "More Hours in My Day, Emilie speaking. How may I help you today?" This is very professional, respectful, and provides the needed information.

→ If you receive a call when you're in the midst of a stressful situation or you're trying to do three things at once, make sure your voice remains calm, upbeat, and cheerful. If possible, ask if you can return the call later in the day.

→ If you work the front desk or are the receptionist, you are the "voice" of the company, the person who makes the company's first impression on a caller. After discerning the caller's needs, transfer the calls quickly and cheerfully. Treat every caller with respect and courtesy.

→ Be considerate of other people's time and don't keep them on hold for a long time.

→ If you receive a call during an appointment or

meeting, tell the caller you're in a meeting and will call him or her as soon as possible.

→ Everyone is very busy, so when you talk on the phone get to the point quickly. Respect the other person's time commitments.

→ When you dial a wrong number, stay on the line and apologize. Don't just hang up. With today's caller ID, the person will know who is calling and you don't want to leave a bad impression.

→ Don't answer someone else's phone or cell phone unless asked to.

→ Return telephone calls and e-mails within 24 hours.

→ When leaving a message, keep it brief. Always leave your name, company name, phone number, and a brief explanation of why you called. Don't go into personal details or leave personal messages on business voice mail.

*All of you should be of one mind.
Sympathize with each other. Love each other
as brothers and sisters. Be tenderhearted,
and keep a humble attitude. Don't repay
evil for evil. Don't retaliate with insults
when people insult you. Instead, pay them
back with a blessing. That is what God has
called you to do, and he will bless you for it.*

APOSTLE PETER

Tea Party Pleasantries

Teatime Delights

*J*ust the thought of a tea party sparks the impression of genteel conversation, delicate manners, and beautiful food presentation, delicious treats, special teas, and Sunday-best dresses. Who can be grumpy or discourteous when room is made at the table, a lovely teapot is placed before them, and delicious delicacies are offered?

Emilie's Inspired Pot Tea

Preparing a perfect cup of tea takes time, but the flavor and excellence is worth it!

⤞ Fill a *teakettle* with five or six cups of freshly drawn cold water. Put the kettle on to boil.

⤞ While the kettle is heating, pour hot water into a *teapot* to warm the inside, which will help keep the tea hot while serving. Ceramic (china, porcelain, stoneware) or glass teapots work best. Tea brewed in metal sometimes has a metallic taste.

✣ Empty the teapot and add a spoonful of loose tea for each cup desired, plus one extra spoonful. (Most teapots hold five to six cups.) If you are using tea bags, use one bag less than the desired number of cups.

✣ As soon as the teakettle water comes to a rolling boil, remove from heat. Overboiling causes the water to lose oxygen, and the resulting brew will taste flat.

✣ Pour boiling water into the teapot, cover, and let the tea brew three to six minutes. Small tea leaves take less time to brew than large ones.

✣ Gently stir the tea before pouring it through a tea strainer and into the teacups. If you used tea bags, remove them.

Caring for the Teapot

The best method is to rinse the teapot with warm water (no soap) and let it air dry. Tannin build-up vanishes when gently scrubbed with a wet cloth dipped in baking soda or by filling the pot with soda and warm water and letting it soak. A lump of sugar in the teapot absorbs moisture and keeps it smelling fresh.

Experiencing a Lovely Tea Party

*W*hen hosting a tea, serving others is the core of the experience. As you think through the menu, the invitation list, and the extra touches you want to add, your heart opens to the joys of hospitality. Whether this is your first tea or you've planned dozens of tea parties, you will delight in the process.

Emilie's Classic Scones

Whether it is middle of winter or the bright beginning of summer, it is perfectly suitable to serve traditional, homemade scones. In fact, it's the polite, delicious thing to do! Here's a great recipe.

> 2 cups flour
>
> 1 tablespoon baking powder
>
> 2 tablespoons sugar
>
> ½ teaspoon salt
>
> 6 tablespoons butter
>
> ½ cup buttermilk (or regular milk)
>
> 1 egg, lightly beaten

1. Mix dry ingredients.

2. Cut in butter until mixture resembles coarse cornmeal.

3. Make a well in the center and pour in butter-milk or regular milk.

4. Mix until dough clings together and is a bit sticky. Don't overmix. (The secret of tender scones is minimum of handling.)

5. Turn out dough onto a floured surface and shape into six- to eight-inch rounds about 1½ inches thick.

6. Quickly cut into pie wedges or use a large, round biscuit cutter to cut circles.

7. Place on ungreased cookie sheet, being sure the sides of scones don't touch.

8. Brush with egg for a shiny, beautiful brown scone.

9. Bake at 425° for 10 to 20 minutes or until light brown.

For variety consider adding:

almond flavoring	cinnamon
apples, diced	cranberries
apricots	currants
blueberries, fresh	ginger
chocolate chips	orange

Bake a selection that suits your guest list. If you're unsure of their likes, a basic, plain scone with a bit of cinnamon and sugar is sure to please. If you have crème fraiche, jams, or compotes available, the options for offerings are unlimited.

Tea Etiquette

→ Bring a small gift for your host.

→ Be punctual, but not early.

→ Cancel only if there is an emergency.

→ Offer to help when needed.

→ Be a good mixer with other guests.

→ If there is a theme to the tea, dress accordingly to add a special touch to the event.

→ Blot your lipstick *before* you sit down at the serving table. You don't want to leave lipstick stains on the teacups.

→ Always turn your cell phone off *before* arriving at the tea.

→ Teas and all liquids are poured beginning with the person on the server's right. The person being served holds her cup in her left hand and extends it toward the server. You may adjust this process if the person receiving is left handed.

→ Scones and crumpets should be eaten in small, bite-sized pieces. If butter, jam, or cream is used, add them to each piece as it is eaten.

→ Proper tea conversation is light and cheery. Good topics include theater, museums, fine arts, music, movies, literature, and travel. Avoid politics, religion, aches and pains, deaths, and other negatives.

→ A knife and fork are usually used with open-faced sandwiches and/or cakes with icing.

→ Milk, cream, and sugar are always added as desired *after* the tea is poured.

→ When leaving the table for a brief period, place the napkin on the seat of the chair. At the end of the tea, the napkin is placed neatly on the table (do not refold).

→ Even if you enjoy talking and socializing, don't be the last to leave.

→ Be sure to say goodbye and thank your host.

→ Always send a handwritten, pleasant thank-you note within 24 hours. (E-mails are not appropriate.)

For additional tea party suggestions, innovations, and themes, see my books *An Invitation to Tea, The Twelve Teas of Inspiration,* and *Friendship Teas to Go.*

Wedding Etiquette

Choosing That Special Ring

When a man and a woman are in love, an engagement often follows...and that means purchasing an engagement ring. Buying the engagement ring falls to the man. Generally speaking the ring includes a diamond, although other gems are also beautiful and suitable. When it comes to choosing a ring, here are some helpful tips.

→ Oftentimes the couple will have discussed and shopped for engagement and wedding rings during their courtship, thus establishing which style of ring is the best match for both of them.

→ Because the man generally purchases the ring as a surprise when he proposes, jewelers generally plan on the need to resize the ring or the possibility of an exchange for a different design. However, the man should be certain of the store's policy *before* he purchases the ring.

→ Keep in mind the taste, lifestyle, and preferences of the bride-to-be. The ring isn't about impressing others, it's a symbol of your love and commitment and her love and commitment to you.

→ Stay within your budget.

→ Make sure the sales receipt states clearly the ring is taken "on approval" and that resizing and exchanges are allowed.

→ Engagement rings are often sold as part of a wedding set. The engagement ring attaches to the wedding ring. After the marriage ceremony the engagement ring is worn above the wedding band.

❦

"We're Engaged!"

The chemistry between a man and woman changes when they announce, "We're going to get married!" Everyone around them knows this couple is serious—no longer just daters. The phones start ringing, the women start planning, and the men can't figure out what everyone is so excited about.

→ The bride's mother usually waits to hear from the man's mother to discuss the upcoming wedding *before* she calls the newspaper to arrange for the announcement to be printed in the paper. During this conversation, they will schedule a time when both sets of parents can get together to talk over the plans for this big life event.

→ In most cases, the bride's mother will take the initiative to get details started since the bride's parents are traditionally responsible for most aspects of the wedding. If the bridegroom's parents are divorced, the protocol should be the same—the bride's mother calls the parents with whom the bridegroom lives. The mother is contacted first, and then the father.

→ If an engagement party is planned, the bride's parents usually are the hosts. However, others may offer to host, and it is appropriate to accept such an offer. This is a great way for both families to meet each other and celebrate the future couple.

Planning the Wedding

The more time and detail you put in at the front end,

the less confusion and stress will occur as you get closer to the date. If your budget permits, consider hiring a wedding coordinator. If you can't afford such a person, check with friends who are married or have helped with other weddings. Do research at the library, online, and interview the gown provider, the caterer, the baker, and so forth. They have vast experience in this area and can offer exceptional insights.

It's very important that mother and daughter are in agreement regarding the process and choices (and consulting the groom is a great idea too). It's also courteous for them to include the groom's mother so she will feel involved. Before you get too far in the planning process you will consider three very important questions:

❖ How formal will the wedding be?

❖ What is the budget?

❖ How many guests will be invited?

Set the boundaries in the very beginning. If you do this, you'll end up with an event that is everything you want it to be. A costly, formal wedding isn't for everyone. A very casual event can be great fun and very romantic when set at the beach, a garden, or at a resort with a small group of family and friends.

The wedding should be a happy experience for everyone, especially the bride, the groom, and their parents.

Engagement and Wedding Announcements

Some people say, "Yes, it's proper to send out printed announcements for the engagement and the wedding," and others say, "No, use the newspaper announcement for both." Think through this delicate matter carefully.

With a newspaper only notice, people don't feel as obligated to send gifts. Also, it avoids possible confusion if engagement invitations are sent out but not everyone who gets an engagement notice will be invited to the actual wedding.

The couple decides what route to go after consulting both sets of parents. If the newspaper option is chosen, the bride and her mother usually furnish the pictures and the written information. This way the information will be accurate, names will be spelled correctly, and you can choose what is shared. Providing this information to the newspaper is best done in person because miscommunication over the phone is a common occurrence. You don't want any errors in the announcement. If the engaged couple or their parents live in a different place than where they've lived for many years, consider running the announcement in the "hometown" newspaper also.

Guest Lists

*T*he wedding day is traditionally known as "the bride's day." And the bride's family is considered the host for this event so they decide the number of guests to be invited. The tricky part is to determine how many, and how to divide the number of guests allowed between the two families. Is it 50/50 or will the host family get to invite more guests than the groom's parents since they are footing the expense? If the groom's side of the wedding wants more invitations than they are allocated, the bride's parents have choices:

→ Give some of their allotment to them to keep the total count within the number that was predetermined.

→ Say no, that they need to work within their number of guests allowed.

→ Say yes and expand the size of the wedding.

→ Say yes but ask the groom's parents to assume the extra costs.

The host family will have to make that decision. In some cases the groom's parents or the couple getting married might be hosting the event. Remember, budget limitations play a major factor in guest list decisions.

Guest List Solutions

→ When budget and size of facility determine how many guests there will be, consider having two lists: those invited to the ceremony only and those invited to the ceremony and the reception afterward. Or have a shorter list of people invited to the wedding ceremony and invite more to the reception. This option is perfect when the church or place where the wedding will be held is small or the couple want to keep the wedding more intimate. If the families attend churches and invite the congregations, they might invite them to the ceremony only and reserve the reception event to immediate family and personal friends.

→ Creating guest lists can be difficult. No one wants to offend family members or friends by leaving someone out. On the other hand, space and budgets are limiting factors. No matter what you decide, someone will probably be offended or omitted. When that happens tell the person you're sorry, remind yourself you can't please everyone, and do the best you can without adding more stress to your life or the process.

Wedding Invitations

The choices on style and expense for invitations are as broad as your budget will allow. You can go from the high end of copperplate engraving etched with fine line lettering to the least expensive method of flat printing. Tastes and expenses vary. If you aren't the bride, be sure to include the engaged couple in wedding-related decisions. The main factors you'll face when choosing invitations are:

→ wording

→ typestyle

→ ink color

→ printing costs

→ whether to have matching envelopes

Printers, books, and websites can provide options for wording to match the type of wedding, such as traditional, divorced parents with joint invitations, a double wedding, a single parent, or a military wedding. Printers will also have samples of wedding invitations you can look at to help make your choices. If there will be a reception or refreshments will be offered, asking invited guests to RSVP is a good idea.

Have several people proof the invitations very carefully (letter by letter). Misprints and typos happen, so be extremely careful. Once you approve the text, you're committed financially even if there are errors.

Sending the Good News

→ Send invitations three to four weeks ahead of time. If you have guests from out of state or foreign countries, more lead time is necessary.

→ Who would think that there is a proper way to stuff an envelope? There is! Picture yourself as the recipient. When you open the invitation, the first thing you should see is your handwritten name on the unsealed inner envelope. So the inner envelope's front faces the front of the outer envelope.

As you carefully turn the unsealed envelope over to withdraw the invitation, the engraved wording should face you. So the inside invitation should face the back of the outer envelope. Any enclosures should be in front of or placed inside the fold of the invitation so they won't be overlooked.

Clergy

→ Selecting the clergy is the responsibility of the

bride and her parents. If the groom would like to have his family's clergy included, find out and make those arrangements early.

→ In most cases the bridegroom pays the clergy's honorarium. Check around your area to see what the recommended amount is. Each denomination has different policies on how weddings are handled. Some feel that such events are part of their ministering to the members of their congregations, while others consider weddings a way to augment their incomes. Some may choose to have the honorarium directed to their churches.

→ If the clergy has to travel to perform the ceremony, the travel expenses, including food, housing, and fuel, are paid by the bridegroom. The couple being married should make sure the clergy know how much their services are appreciated.

The Marriage License

Good manners also involves taking care of important details responsibly. As a couple prepares for their wedding, official matters are crucial, including getting the marriage license. Every state has specific requirements for obtaining the license. Check with your local officials to see what is needed and when. Without a marriage license, you won't be legally married. Some requirements to meet before filing the license will probably be:

- ⇢ proof of legal age to be married (marriage is a contract) or parental consent to be married

- ⇢ proof of required medical tests

- ⇢ other requirements met, such as a waiting period

- ⇢ that both parties are single, widowed, or divorced (bigamy and polygamy are illegal)

- ⇢ proof that the person officiating the wedding can lawfully conduct the ceremony

- ⇢ the signatures of the bride, groom, and two witnesses to prove the wedding was voluntary and that it took place

Wedding Expenses

$\mathcal{T}$raditionally, the bride's parents pay for the wedding. The thinking behind this concept was that the groom was taking on the expense of a wife and family. However, today brides have careers and contribute to household expenses. Now many couples make arrangements with both sets of parents to offset the wedding expenses. And some couples take on the expense themselves. However, it's wise never to assume anything when it comes to finances.

Soon after the engagement, the couple should sit down and create a list of what they want and don't want for the wedding. They need to make a list of wedding needs and discuss them openly, including hearing any concerns about the costs and family responsibilities. Then they need to get with both sets of parents (separately at first) to discuss what is expected and what can be anticipated. Talking money isn't a favorite activity for most folks, but this discussion can be pleasant and unite the families in a common goal.

Every wedding situation is unique, but here are a few general guidelines:

The Bride's Expenses

→ groom's ring

→ gift for groom

→ physical examination and blood test

→ stationery for thank-you notes

→ gift for the maid of honor and bridesmaids

Bride's Family Expenses

→ invitations and wedding announcements

→ wedding consultant

→ ceremony expenses, including location rental and deposits

→ flowers for the ceremony and bridesmaid bouquets. Some traditions have the groom pay for the bride's bouquet and going-away corsage

→ wedding dress

→ bridesmaids' luncheon

→ photography and videography services

→ guest book, ring bearer's pillow, and other incidental items

→ transportation for wedding party to the ceremony

→ accommodations for out-of-town members of the bride's wedding party

The Groom's Expenses

→ bride's engagement and wedding rings

→ marriage license

→ physical examination and blood test

→ boutonnieres for father and male attendants

→ bride's bouquet and going-away corsage

→ flowers for both mothers and grandmothers

→ clothing accessories (ties, ascots) for male attendants

→ gift for the bride

→ gifts for ushers and best man

→ bachelor dinner—optional

The Groom's Family Expenses

→ fee for person officiating the wedding

→ transportation for the bridal couple to the wedding and reception

→ honeymoon expenses (unless received as a wedding gift)

→ family's travel expenses

→ accommodations for out-of-town attendants

→ wedding gift to the couple

→ wedding rehearsal dinner

Bridesmaid and Best Man/Usher Expenses

→ wedding clothes

→ travel costs

➢ individual gift to the couple or sharing
expenses for a present from each group of
attendants

Gifts for Attendants and Parents

The bride pays for her bridesmaids' gifts and the
groom pays for his attendants' gifts. These gifts are gestures of appreciation for helping to make the wonderful occasion memorable. They need to be personal but
not necessarily costly. Many stores will give discounts for
buying several gifts at a time. Here are a few gift ideas:

FOR WOMEN

➢ perfume

➢ earrings

➢ bracelet

➢ necklace

➢ pewter picture frame

FOR MEN

➢ money clip

➢ tie clasp

➢ leather wallet

→ pen and pencil set

→ desk clock

→ business card holder

The maid/matron of honor and the best man should receive slightly more expensive gifts since their duties for the day are more involved.

Parent Gifts

The couples give both sets of parents token gifts in appreciation for all they've done to raise them and for their participation in this major event in their lives. If you plan to purchase the presents during your honeymoon, mention this to both sets of parents.

Wedding Gifts

Giving Gifts

→ Gifts are a token of goodwill, affection, and commitment. Just because you're invited to a lavish wedding doesn't mean you have to give a lavish gift. Always give within your means.

→ Gifts should be sent to the bride's home before

the wedding. After the wedding, gifts can be
sent or taken to the new couple's home or to
the bride's parents' home. If possible, avoid taking gifts to the wedding because they'll have to
be moved on the day of the wedding, and there
are already plenty of details being handled.

Receiving Wedding Gifts

→ Gifts are best opened privately by the bride
and groom to avoid guests feeling badly about
their gifts if they compare them to what others
sent and if there are duplicates. (The amount
spent on each gift varies because of the budget restraints of the givers.) Save the enjoyable
gift-opening task for a special time as husband
and wife. Some couples open gifts in the presence of their parents if a lot of friends of the
family attended and brought presents.

→ Remember to keep a detailed list of what you
received and who gave the items to you so you
can properly thank people.

→ Returning or exchanging wedding gifts should
be handled discreetly. If the gifts you want to
exchange are from people who will be visiting your home and would notice the absence

of their gifts, discuss exchanging the gifts with them. If the gift is from someone you won't be entertaining in your home, feel free to exchange it. This also holds true for duplicate gifts.

As the Big Day Comes to a Close

The grand day has to wind down at some point. Eventually it's time to think about leaving the reception and going on the honeymoon, if one is planned. There doesn't seem to be any set rules for the reception and when the new couple leaves. Some couples might prefer to be the last ones to leave and others might have planes to catch for their honeymoons.

→ The party isn't over just because the new husband and wife need to leave. The parents can excuse themselves for a few minutes so they can say their goodbyes, and then they can return for the rest of the festivities.

→ Often the best man signals that the bride and groom will be departing in a few minutes. Those wishing to assemble form two rows for the bride and groom to walk between on the way to their getaway car. At this time rice or birdseed can be tossed by friends and family who are cheering and clapping and sending the couple off in style.

→ Many newlyweds stay in a local hotel for the first night rather than travel after such a hectic day. They don't tell very many people where they are staying unless they want company.

Saying Thank You

→ Thank-you notes for engagement party gifts should be sent out within two to three weeks. Wedding thank-you notes should go out within two months after you return from the honeymoon.

→ Using the gift list you made while opening the presents, write your thank-you notes. Check each name off when you seal the thank-you card's envelope.

→ Thank-you notes should be handwritten. To make the notes more personal, you can include appreciation for any extra effort the people made to attend your wedding, such as traveling, helping out, or if it was just wonderful to see them.

→ Thank-you notes should include the specific item you're thanking them for. If you've used the gift, mention how much you enjoyed it. Or you can say why you like the gift. If people sent gifts but weren't able to attend, thank them for thinking of you on your special day. Expressing your heartfelt gratitude is your gift to the gift giver.

→ Traditionally the bride was responsible for the thank-you notes, but making this a joint couple endeavor makes the experience more enjoyable, reminds both of you what you received and from whom, and gets the job done more quickly.

*Friends and good manners will
carry you where money won't go.*

MARGARET WALKER

Emilie Barnes

To contact Emilie Barnes, to find out more about "More Hours in My Day" time management and organization seminars, or to buy "More Hours in My Day" organization products, visit:

www.EmilieBarnes.com

write to

More Hours in My Day
2150 Whitestone Dr.
Riverside, CA 92506

or call

951-682-4714

To learn more about Emilie's books and read sample chapters, visit www.harvesthousepublishers.com.

More Great Books from Emilie Barnes

Good Manners for Today's Kids

Bestselling authors Bob and Emilie Barnes encourage families to build strong foundations of good manners and godly behavior. With biblical wisdom, proven advice, great examples, and drawing on personal experiences, they will help you teach your young children to communicate confidently, respect others and God, and practice good manners and thoughtfulness throughout the day.

Quiet Moments Alone with God

In this thoughtful book, much-loved author and home-management expert Emilie Barnes helps you develop consistent devotional habits. Each 15-minute quiet moment includes a Scripture verse, a brief devotion, and an inspiring message.

The Quick-Fix Home Organizer

Organizational expert Emilie Barnes is known for her decorative style, common sense, and practical advice in all areas of home management. In this helpful book she offers easy-to-implement, creative, and inspirational ideas to help you create a home filled with peace and personality.